Know-So Money
Hope-So Money

*Retirement Secrets Wall Street Doesn't
Want You to Know*

by

Stephen J. Kelley, CSA

Safety First Financial Planners
33 Main Street, Suite 201
Nashua, NH 03064

603-881-8811

Safety
First
Financial Planners

www.FreeMoneyGuys.com

Table of Contents

Warning:

I should point out right up front that much of this booklet deals with Fixed Index Annuities (FIA) and life insurance, so if you have some kind of weird aversion to them, you can stop reading right now.

Still reading? Okay, then let me make one thing very clear...we are not wedded to annuities or life insurance.

We are wedded to the results.

The fact is you can do things with annuities and life insurance that you cannot do with any other product or investment on the market. Period. Here are just a few You can:

- Receive *market-like returns* with no (zero, zip, nada) risk to your principal and accrued interest.

- Ensure *guaranteed income for the rest of your life* at a higher rate than with any other investment—*without giving up control of your money.*

- *Reduce taxes* on your investment savings to under 2%.

- *Reduce or eliminate the taxes* you pay on your Social Security taxes.

- Completely remove your IRA/401(k) from your estate, passing 100% of your beginning balance to your heirs *tax free* while enjoying greater income than provided by your RMD.

- Provide all of these benefits (and more) with *no fees or risk*.

See why we like them? Not because they are annuities and life insurance (we are fully licensed planners...if other things did what these do we would be recommending them!), but *because they give you results you can't get anywhere else. They are the ultimate "Know-So Money."*

VAs: A Wolf in Sheep's Clothing

We often get the questions, "So why hasn't my broker recommended them?" or "Why doesn't my advisor like them?"

We believe it's because they don't really understand them. Whenever we have the opportunity to introduce a broker, money manager, CPA or other planner to these products (and we have trained thousands over the years!), we find that they readily adopt and start to recommend them.

Another reason is that most planners are stock brokers, and are constrained by what their "broker/dealers" permit them to sell. Most broker/dealers do not like fixed products...they like securities. They are creatures of Wall Street. They work for big Wall Street firms, so it stands to reason that the products they sell and the recommendations they make are commissioned Wall Street recommendations: risk-based "Hope-So Money."

So, if they do think about annuities, they think about variable annuities (VA), with which many people have had bad experiences. So some planners do tend to stay away from annuities altogether. In our minds they are right about VAs.

In fact, you should know that almost any time a broker, planner, newspaper, television pundit, magazine article, or your neighborhood barber refers to annuities, they are talking about **variable annuities**. In fact unless they specifically say "fixed annuity," or "immediate annuity," or some other descriptive qualification, you should assume they are referring to variable annuities.

How do variable annuities differ from those we use? Simple, really. When you invest money in a variable annuity you are actually hiring the insurance company to invest your money in the stock market for you. In other words, you are paying a third party to put your money at risk for an extra, and quite substantial, fee.

Fees, Fees, and More Fees

So, in addition to all the normal management fees and commissions (many of them hidden) that you would normally pay in a mutual fund, you are adding administrative fees, surrender charges, and other hidden fees for the insurance company. And you are no safer than you would have been. In fact, all you have done is put one more layer of bureaucracy between you and your money.

Here is an example of the fees you would incur in a typical variable annuity:

- Administration fees, charged by insurance companies to administer your accounts typically run ½-1% per year. Administer...not manage. Administer means moving your money around when you call and tell them to.

- Life insurance fees that guarantee the premium amount if you die typically run 1%-2% per year.

- Mutual fund fees run ½-2% annually. Most people are better off buying funds directly than paying an insurance company fees to administer and paying ordinary income tax on the gains.

- Rider fees can be very high and provide dubious benefits at best. These fees often run 2% or more per year.

That means *fees on a $100,000 investment will run from $2,500 to $7,000 per year whether you make money or not.*

Think about that. **If you hold $100,000 in a variable annuity for 10 years, your only guarantee is that you will pay out $25,000 to $70,000 in fees. Whether you make any money or not!**

Dubious Advantages

But what about those guarantees and other advantages variable annuities are always hyping?

The benefits to the investor are marginal if they exist at all. I recently had a woman come in to discuss her mom's variable annuity. Her broker had told her that the value of the account (which originally had $100,000 deposited into it) was really $125,000, even though her statement said it was worth only $70,000. She thought the $125,000 was correct because she had been told there was a 5% minimum guarantee on the annuity.

So we called the company. This is something I often do when meeting with clients because it is so enlightening to them. Also, I know what questions to ask! What we found out was that if her mom died, she would receive $125,000. But if her mom wanted to take her money out today, she would only get $70,000!

What was she paying for that benefit? $1,000 per year. For what was essentially a life insurance policy (maybe) worth $55,000. And she was sold this annuity as a safe investment, even though her total $100,000 was at risk in the market, unless she died! <u>Bottom line, she was sold an unnecessarily risky investment and then charged an expensive fee to mitigate a portion of that risk available to her only after she died.</u>

In another case I had a prospective client tell me he had a variable annuity that had a minimum annual growth of 6%. This is a very popular annuity from a major life insurance company that is marketed to millions of people as a safe investment with a guaranteed rate of return of 6%. So once again we called the company and found out that in order to get the advantage of the 6%, he would have to draw income from his annuity over his lifetime. If he ever wanted to access the actual money in the

3

annuity, he would have to take the money from the funds that had shrunk substantially over the years, less annual fees of about 3.5%.

So, once again, a needlessly and inappropriately risky investment that charged a fee to mitigate a portion of the risk that should have never been taken in the first place.

Needless to say he was quite unhappy to learn the truth.

But What About the Tax Benefits?

This is one where we've really been sold a bill of goods. Remember the old "tax deferred annuity"? Well you don't hear so much about that any more. Here's why. Annuities ARE tax-deferred, that's correct. However when you finally do pay taxes on them you pay ordinary income tax, not the much lower capital gains taxes you pay on stocks and some mutual funds.

Back in the day, when VAs were initially introduced, this wasn't a big deal, because capital gains taxes were the same as ordinary income tax. So tax deferral had some advantages.

Now, however, tax deferral can be a real problem, because you are not only deferring the taxes, but the tax rate as well. Variable annuities only serve to exacerbate the problem because they effectively eliminate all of the tax advantages of holding a long term investment: long term capital gains. So you end up paying higher taxes on more money.

Here is a quote from Jane Bryant Quinn of Newsweek on variable annuities: "You rarely find me so deeply angry at a common investment product that I dream of blowing it to smithereens..... My target: tax-deferred, variable annuities.

And, from John Biggs, former chair of TIAA-CREF pension funds, *the creator of VAs*: "I cannot imagine a personal financial situation where I'd recommend a VA (variable annuity) as a good idea."

4

In a nutshell, our objections to variable annuities are:

- High risk
- High fees
- High surrender charges
- Limited investment options
- Long surrender periods
- Elimination of long term capital gains
- The need to add expensive riders to eliminate their core problem—risky investments dressed up like safe money instruments (Hope-So Money!).

Don't get me wrong. I don't hate the markets or risk. I own my own Registered Investment Advisory firm, Coach Capital Management! I just think your risk-growth money is better invested directly in the market...your options are greater, you have no surrender charges or periods, and fees are much lower (total fees for people who invest with us, including management fees and underlying fund costs: 1.6%!).

But if what you want is a safe money instrument that can give you guaranteed income for the rest of your life, why not just go with the product that was designed that way from the ground up?

It's kind of like buying a very fast and expensive sports car to haul your family of eight kids around. You'd have to stretch it out, add a bunch of seats and other safety equipment to do the job.

That doesn't mean sports cars are bad—they're just not right for a family wagon. Buy a van to carry the kids, and buy a sports car to tool around on the weekends.

Buy a safe money product for your income, and invest directly in the markets for your growth. Don't try to combine the two; it's very expensive and doesn't work!

Hybrids: Not Your Father's Annuities

So that brings us back to the annuities we DO like; the new breed of **Hybrid Annuities**. You should know right off the top that these are not variable annuities, nor are they the same as the fixed annuities that were available just over a decade ago. Or the traditional immediate annuity that requires you to trade away your money for income. In fact they are a hybrid of the three. An annuity contract that takes the best of the three and leaves the worst behind. Most important, they are safe, Know-So Money.

The market has changed dramatically since the 90s and the insurance industry has caught up in a big way. The primary differences between now and then has to do with the way the new generation of retirees and pre-retirees think of their money.

Our parents were brought up on the idea of the defined benefits plan. It was based on the idea that they contributed during their working lives and when they retired they got a specific benefit...pension, healthcare, etc., for the rest of their lives. They really never related to the pool of money funding it; they were more concerned about the ongoing security they received.

Our generation was brought up on the modern 401(k) which began in 1980 *and shifted the risk, and burden of management, onto the retiree.* It also shifted trillions of dollars into Wall Street's pockets, causing the run-ups in the market over the 80s and 90s, and making a lot of Wall Street people and bankers very, very rich, and decimated millions of retirement plans in the process.

The result: instead of watching the end game...or the benefits, we were taught to keep our eye on the pool of money being accumulated. We were taught to watch rates of return, risk tolerance, and a bunch of other stuff that really has nothing to do with retirement planning.

So the old fashioned annuity that concentrated on lifetime payouts and benefits through annuitization no longer fit the model, because they required the retiree to commit their money to the annuity, thereby losing control of it. In effect, committing what we call "annuicide."

We now needed a newer model that allowed people to keep control of their money. But the benefits of lifetime payouts and the security it brings to retirees is still very valuable. So, the industry came up with a whole new line of annuities that met both needs: the need to keep control of one's money, and the need for excellent and safe returns and guaranteed lifetime income streams that could only be provided by annuities.

Enter the modern **Fixed Index Annuity, a.k.a., The Hybrid Annuity**. We call it "the have your cake and eat it too annuity." Try this on for size:

1. It's completely, 100% safe. You cannot lose a dime of your principal or any accrued interest unless you pull your money out before the surrender period is over.

   Okay, now wait a minute. Weren't surrender periods and charges one of the main reasons you objected to variable annuities a little earlier? Yes, they were. And here's why...they didn't buy you anything! Hold on and I will explain. In the mean time, back to the advantages of the FIA:

2. They allow you to receive market-like gains without market risk (see the section on eliminating market risk later in this book).

3. They provide superior, guaranteed, lifetime income you cannot outlive without giving up control of your money.

4. You pay no fees or commissions out of your money (unless you add certain benefits, and then you pay a SMALL fee).

5. They have excellent liquidity: you can always have access to 10% (or sometimes more) of your money per year with ZERO surrender charges. If you need more, some contracts allow you to get up to 100% of your principal with no penalties to principal; only interest. If you die, end up in a nursing home or become terminally ill, the whole amount is always paid out without penalty.

6. When used properly, they can provide huge tax advantages.

Okay, now back to our point about surrender periods and charges. Unless surrender charges are buying you something they are not good. *With a Fixed Index Annuity, the surrender charge is buying you something.* It's buying complete safety, market like returns without the risk, no fees, lifetime income without giving up control of your money and potentially huge tax advantages. None of these things is available with the VAs, and yet you still have surrender charges, as well as huge fees. So that's why we object to them.

Protection from Stock Market Losses

One of the main issues today's retirees have is losses in the market. Indeed, many have called the first decade of the 21st Century the "Lost Decade." If you had held your money just in the S&P500 from January 1, 2001 until the end of the decade, you would have averaged just a -3.1% average return on your money!

The picture doesn't get much better over the longer term. If you started in 1990 and held it until last year you would have made on average about 5.3% average return. If you net fees (average 2% and taxes out of that, you barely kept up with inflation...the one thing that the market is supposed to do for you!).

But somehow people never believe me when I show them these figures...after all it goes against everything they "know." One of my favorite sayings is by Mark Twain, writing for the slave, Jim, from *Huckleberry Finn*: "It ain't what we don't know that gives us trouble, it's what we know for certain that just ain't so."

So consider this from DALBAR's 2008 Quantitative Analysis: "The typical mutual fund investor has actually been losing money every year for the last 20 years, after adjusting for inflation."

Or this one from the May/June 2009 issue of the Journal of Indexes: "For the past forty years, ordinary long-term treasury bonds have outpaced investing in the stock market, which means the only 'rewards' investors have received for taking the extra risk of stocks and equity mutual funds are sleepless nights and broken retirement dreams."

So, okay. We know that the conventional approach has problems (just remember the lost decade for confirmation). But what can you do about it?

Benjamin Franklin is reputed to have said, "The definition of insanity is doing the same thing over and over again and expecting different results." Think about this quote for a second and ask yourself, does this apply to the way you manage your money?

For many people it does. They get so caught up in fear and greed cycle that they just keep on repeating the same patters. And by way of "comforting" themselves in down times, they say, "Well, everyone else has lost money, too."

The truth is everyone else hasn't lost money. Your broker hasn't. He or she makes money whether or not you do (when was the last time you got out of paying fees and commissions just because you lost some money? The mavens on Wall Street haven't. They fly around in private jets paid for by your 401(k). Members of Congress haven't. They get big donations from Wall Street to keep things going the way they are. The corporate media haven't. They get advertising revenues from those very same people to keep the hoax going.

Am I saying these people are all Madoffs and out to get you? Not at all. All I am saying is the system has been so tilted in their favor for so long that it led inexorably to the melt down that crashed the housing market, put eight million people out of work, and overnight wiped out trillions in retirement savings and wealth. You might want to get off this train before it is too late.

It isn't too late. If you stuck with it you should have recovered all you lost, so now might be a great time to reposition some of your assets into Know-So Money. Not only did the above not lose money in the meltdown; nor did the millions of people who have discovered the Fixed Indexed Annuity. This is a wonderful new concept, created by the insurance industry during the 1990s to compete with the soaring stock market. And compete it has. So much so that the SEC actually tried to take them over so they could be regulated out of existence, until it was slapped down by Congress and the courts.

So exactly what are they and why are they important to you? FIAs provide you with a portion of the market upside with none of the downside.

Consider this quote by Donald Trump from *The Art of the Deal*: "As long as the basic concept remained intact—no downside for me and a 50% share in the upside—it was an extraordinary deal."

This is the basis of what fixed indexed annuities do for you...they completely eliminate the downside and give you a portion (often the lion's share) of the upside of the stock market with no market risk whatsoever.

Here's how it works. The interest rate the annuity pays you is tied to a market index, such as the S&P 500. You should know that all FIAs limit what you can earn (but remember they eliminate risk). So they may have a cap, a spread, a participation rate or some other mechanism to limit their payouts. *This is not done to skim profit off the top, it is a necessary component of the mechanism that makes these possible.* We will fully explain this to you if you wish to pursue this further.

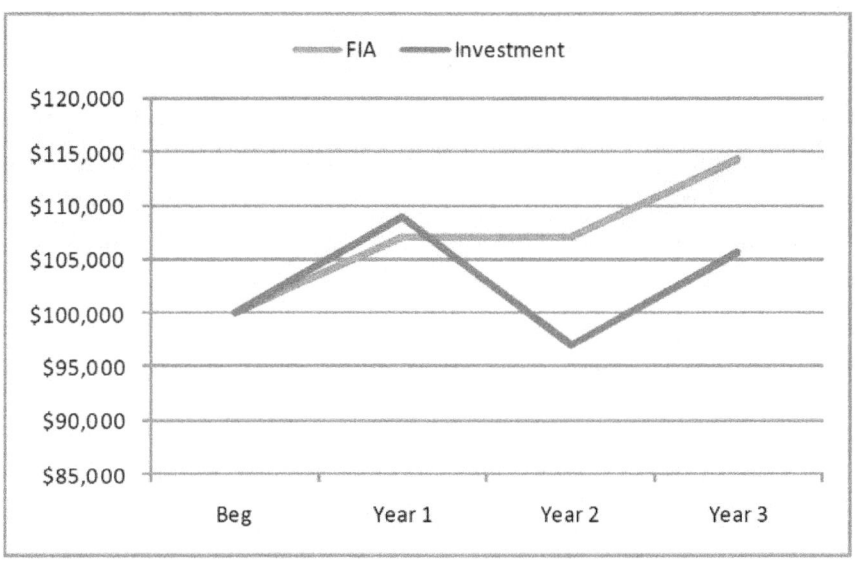

Looking at the above chart, assume that you started in an annuity when the S&P 500 was at 500, and the annuity has a 7% cap (this is the maximum payout for the year).

After year one it's the S&P 500 is at 550 for a 10% increase. The investment starts at $100,000. The FIA goes up by 7%, the full amount provided by the cap. The investment fund (market) went up by 8.9%, the amount of the index increase less the 1.1% fee.

During the second year the market fell by 10%. Now logically, the investment fund should be showing even, but remember there are fees charged...whether you make or lose money. Plus the 10% loss was on the full amount, not just the original $100,000. Therefore the investment fund is now in negative territory at $97,030.

However the FIA is still showing $107,000 due to the annual reset. Now the market goes up 10% again in year three. The investment fund starts at $97,030, goes up 10% (minus 1.1% fees) and ends up at $105,762. But the annuity, because of the annual reset, starts at $107,000. So even though it only gets 70% of the upside, it got NONE of the downside and is way ahead of the market.

Now you are off and running. The investment fund will have a very difficult time ever catching up with the annuity.

But wait...what about the caps? What if the market goes up 30% and I have a cap of 7%? Well, that can happen. But that's where a good advisor that understands these policies comes into play, because there are many "crediting strategies" available. Some use caps, some use participation rates (ex. 50% of the upside), some use spreads (100% of everything after the first 3-5%). There are annual point to point, monthly average, monthly point to point, etc.

The thing to remember is that you have lots of options to maximize your gain, and we can help you with that. But, unlike in a securities investment, you have NO RISK of losing any money. So,

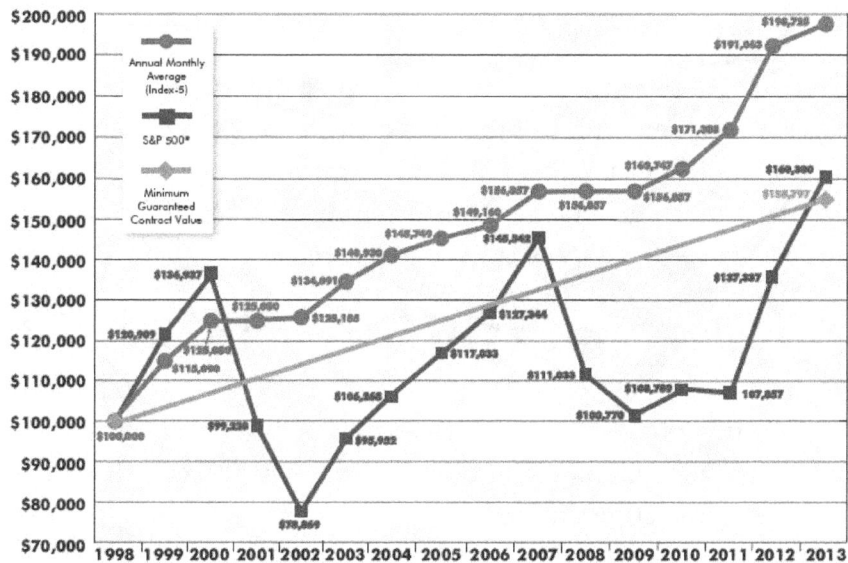

if we guess wrong, you might make 12% interest one year instead of 15%. But if your broker guesses wrong, you could LOSE 30% of your holdings!

Above is an actual chart comparing the S&P 500 and one of our favorite FIA crediting strategies during the 15 year period from 1998 to the end of 2013. The light blue line shows the minimum guaranteed value of the contract, which is 2% (the same gains you would have had in the market during that 15 year period).

Note how the FIA way out-performed the S&P 500. When the market went up, so did the FIA. However, when it went down, all principal and profits were locked in. No market risk and great return, with all the safety of CDs.

This is why we like these plans. Because they provide an outcome that is nearly ideal for the client, and for us. (Happy clients!)

How Safe is Safe?

Fixed annuities and life insurance contracts emphasize safety above everything else. In fact, financial experts consider fixed annuities and life insurance, CDs and treasuries as the safest monetary instruments available. And of the three, fixed life insurance products have by far the very best track record.

Now I know how that sounds. Please just read on and I will explain why that is.

People often wonder if annuities are FDIC insured? And the answer is no, they are not. But they actually have a better record of depositor protection in the event of company failure than the FDIC.

How can this be?

Fixed insurance and annuity policies are protected by the **Legal Reserve System.** The Legal Reserve System dictates and enforces very strict controls and safety measures on how money under its oversight is managed.

Why is FDIC Insurance necessary?

Banks can have up to a nine-to-one ratio of liabilities to capital. Here's what that means. If you deposit $1,000 in a bank, the bank can go to the Federal Reserve and borrow up to $9,000 against that $1,000. Then, the bank can lend that money out to personal loans, credit cards, run businesses, and all of the other commercial lending activities a bank engages in.

They get in trouble, however, when they start to get greedy like what happened during the years prior to 2008 when they started lending to financial markets and investing in derivatives and all kinds of things commercial banks were never supposed to do. Before we knew it, they were swimming in mountains of debt they couldn't pay back and the whole system came down.

Obviously, banks can easily become over-leveraged, and sometimes in very risky investments, like those that led to the recent financial and banking crisis of 2008, and the Great Depression of the 1930s. FDIC insurance is critical for safety and protecting depositors from a financial meltdown like happened in the 30s. However, as we saw in 2008, even these measures were not enough to prevent another catastrophe.

Why the Legal Reserve System is Different

First, Legal Reserve life insurance companies are legally prohibited from speculating with your money. Unlike banks, markets or any other financial system, 100% of their investment of your money must, by law, be invested in the very safest monetary vehicles available.

Most goes into long-term investment-grade bonds, treasuries, and extremely conservative real estate and other types of commercial developments.

Second, life insurance companies are required by law to maintain a greater than one-to-one ratio of their capital to their liabilities. If they bring in a dollar, unlike banks, they cannot lend nine, or six, or three, or even one dollar. They can lend out (invest) only what is left over after the reserve fund is set aside.

A large percentage of each premium dollar calculated by actuaries for each company goes into the *policy owner's reserve fund*. This policy reserve (Legal Reserve) fund is a liability to the life insurance company. The fund is established as a way of determining or measuring the assets the company must maintain in order to be able to meet its future commitments under the policies it has issued. In other words, the reserve liabilities are established as financial safeguards to ensure the company will have sufficient assets to pay its claims and other commitments when they fall due. These assets are kept intact for payment of living and death benefits to the insured. In other words, the insurance company isn't backing your money, your *money* is!

If an insurance company's reserve levels fall short and it is unable to correct the situation, it goes into what is called receivership. The remaining insurance companies in the state legal reserve pool must assume the liabilities and obligations of the insurer. The reserve pool protects fixed annuity investors as well as those who purchase other life insurance products or policies.

Third, Legal Reserve Life Insurers are members of reinsurance groups. If you purchase an annuity from Company A, Company A has secured agreements from Companies B, C, and D to help cover its liabilities. Each company has from four to a dozen other companies backing its contracts.

Fourth, insurance companies don't have to comply just with one governing body like banks, they must satisfy the safety requirements of all 50 states. Every year all legal reserve life insurance companies submit annual statements to the insurance departments of each state in which they are licensed to do business. These are detailed reports of an insurance company's financial status that is important in evaluating the company's solvency and compliance with the insurance laws. Companies found not to comply with their reserve requirements have their operations suspended immediately and are prohibited from selling more policies until they have taken corrective action.

In the unlikely event that a company's annual statement or its own examination reveals possible financial weakness, one of several avenues is open to the company:

- Produce additional operating capital;
- Sell its business to another life company;
- Merge into another financially stable life company.

A legal reserve life insurance company does not simply close its doors and go out of business declaring that all policies are null and void. Legal reserve life policyholders enjoy personal security safeguards unknown by other type of financial industry.

Fifth, if one company is purchased or merged into another, there is no change whatsoever in the policy benefits or premiums. Your contract would be just as binding on the new company as it was on the company you originally purchased it from.

So, the bottom line is in order to lose any money in a fixed life insurance or annuity policy due to company insolvency, ALL of the following would have to happen.

1. Your insurance company's very safe bond portfolio would have to fail.

2. Your surplus fund would have to be depleted.

3. The very safe bond portfolios of all four to 14 reinsurance partners would have to fail, along with their reserve funds.

4. The state reserve fund would have to fail.

5. There would have to be no company left that could merge with the failing company, i.e., a complete financial meltdown far worse than anything we have ever seen before.

This confluence of events has never happened in the history of the Legal Reserve System.

I promised proof at the beginning of this section that the Legal Reserve System had a better track record than the FDIC.

Legal Reserve companies had their strongest showing of strength during the Great Depression of 1929-1938 when some 9,000 banks suspended operations *while 99% of all fixed life insurance in force continued unaffected.*

Many people are not aware that it was not the government that bailed out the banking industry during the Great Depression; it was the U.S. insurance industry. Without it, we would never have pulled out of the Great Depression with our financial system intact. People often question this statement as it is not well publicized. Here are the facts. According to the U.S. Department of Commerce, during the time of the Great Depression the insurance industry pumped over $18 billion into the nation's economy. If you adjust the dollars based on percentage of GDP, using the average GDP of the 10 years of the Great Depression, that equates to around *three to six trillion* in today's dollars! At the same time its assets and ability to pay actually increased from:

1929..................................$18,010,000,000

1934..................................$23,334,308,702

Representing a gain of $ 5,324,308,702

The FDIC is a government agency tasked with insuring depositors against the over-leveraging that is at the core operating principle of the American banking system, and which caused the crash of the thirties and later the 2000s. During the 30s the insurance industry rescued the United States economy. During the crash of 2008 when hundreds of banks failed (in spite of FDIC insurance) most insurance carriers had their ratings reaffirmed by the ratings agencies. *And once again, not one person in a fixed annuity or life policy lost a dime in the melt down.*

Even AIG, which was at the heart of much of the problem with its plan to corner the market on credit default swaps, had its life and annuity division's (American General Life) ratings reaffirmed. In fact they wanted to raid the $400 billion in capitalization they had in reserve to rescue the parent company, but the state insurance departments and federal government would not allow it, since the money belonged not to AIG, but to the policy holders who had taken out the insurance.

The truth is, the United States insurance system is the most secure financial system on earth with over one trillion dollars in reserve capitalization. It is far more solvent than the U.S. Government and U.S. banking system combined. FDIC insurance was created in response to the bank failures of the 1930s. It did not include the insurance industry because there was no need; it already had the proven safeguards of the Legal Reserve System in place.

Had the banking industry complied by these same safeguards, there may never have been a Great Depression, and we would certainly not have gone through the problems of 2008.

You don't have to take our word for it. Even Ben Bernanke, former Chairman of the Federal Reserve and the man in charge of the United States government's monetary policy, understands how safe these policies are. He has most of his retirement plan invested in annuities. If anyone should understand what is safe and what isn't he should!

Double or Triple Your CD Rates

This heading represents a bit of literary license, because we really can't double the rates you get on your CDs. However we can provide the same safety as a CD, and give you much greater return over time than you would get on a CD.

Another advantage of the annuity is the way it's taxed. You don't pay any taxes on it until you actually withdraw the money. When you do withdraw it, you are allowed to recover your initial investment tax free, so you only pay taxes on the growth.

This can save you a lot of money over time. Many people just keep on rolling CDs over year after year. I knew one woman who had over $1 million in CDs. She was not only getting substandard returns on those CDs, but she was paying taxes every year on the "income," even though she just kept on rolling them over.

This killed her on her taxes, and caused her to max out the taxes on her Social Security income. But she just couldn't see her way to moving her money around, and that cost her plenty.

The moral of the story is be cautious...that's okay and appropriate when you are getting older and can't afford to lose any money. But don't be overly cautious to the point where you end up hurting yourself. If you can get a better rate, improve your tax situation, and maintain the safety of your investment, then perhaps you should seriously look at making a change.

We are available to answer any questions you may have regarding any of these matters.

Reduce or Eliminate the Tax on Your Social Security Benefits

Prior to 1984, Social Security income was tax-free. Today, however, taxpayers could be paying tax on up to 85% of their Social Security income. The good news is that annuities can help reduce and sometimes eliminate the income tax on your Social Security income!

The IRS calculates the tax on your Social Security income based on your total income from all sources. However, income you earn on an annuity that is left to accumulate does not appear on your current tax return.

This is different from other financial instruments. Even tax-free bonds, while free of tax, are reported as income on your tax return. You don't pay taxes on them, but they can raise your provisional income rate and income tax bracket; the very things that cause your other taxes and taxes on Social Security income to go up.

Therefore, annuities may reduce your total income for Social Security benefit taxation purposes. In fact, if you shelter enough income in annuities and bring your income below the thresholds (adjusted gross income of $25,000 for a single taxpayer and $32,000 for a married taxpayer) you then pay no tax on your Social Security income at all! This is one of our favorite tax strategies.

Do you want to see if these calculations work to your advantage? Bring in a copy of your tax return (including Schedule B) to our offices. We should be able to let you know how much you could save in taxes.

Pass your IRA/401(k) to your spouse, children and grandkids while maintaining its tax-deferred status

One of our favorite strategies is one we call an Individual Pension Account (IPA™). **It lets you take a maximum amount of income while you are alive, and leave 100% of your IRA to your heirs...tax free!**

Taxes on qualified money can be as much as 66%. The primary taxes are Estate and Inheritance Taxes, Income Taxes, and Income Taxes In Respect to the Decedent (IRD). That last is a fancy way of saying that if you don't pay the taxes while you are alive, your children will have to after you are gone. And most often, at a higher rate. You can offset the IRD and Inheritance Taxes against each other, so be sure to take that up with your advisor.

How does the IPA™ help?

Consider the example on the next page. Assume your IRA is worth $250,000 and you are 70 ½ years old, and you are now forced to take the required minimum distribution (RMD), whether you want it or not. You may not realize that if you abide by the RMD tables as mandated by federal tax statute, you will be forced to take the most income at age 93 when you are apt to need it the least. Then, when you do finally pass it along to your heirs, they will be forced to pay taxes on their inheritance (and it can also raise the stakes for any other death taxes you may incur).

The first section in the calculator shows the impact of the IPA™ after year one. Income with the Required Minimum Distribution (RMD) is $9,124, but the IPA™ provides $14,764 (61% more). If death occurred now, $250,000 goes to heirs, but under the traditional IRA, there is an IRD tax of $93,431 plus any state

IPA™ (a.k.a. IRA 590™) plan compared to traditional IRA

Individual Pension Account (IPA™) Calculator

Enter Your Age:	70	Enter your age, the amount of your	
Enter the Size of Your IRA:	$250,000	qualified funds, and your sex. The cal-	
Your Sex:	Male	culator will show you the impact an IRA 590™ could have on your retirement.	

	Traditional IRA	Income4Life IRA 590™	Advantage or Disadvantage
Year One			
Annual Income:	$9,124	$14,764	**61.81%** — More income now and guaranteed for life with the IRA 590™
Death Benefit:	$250,000	$250,000	**100.00%** — Equal amounts go to heirs at the beginning of withdrawals
Tax paid by heirs:	$93,431		**$93,431** — More goes to heirs. The IRA 590™ passes to heirs completely tax free.
To Heirs After Tax:	$156,569	$250,000	**59.67%** — More value from the very beginning!
Life Expectancy Age 82			
Annual Income:	$13,736	$14,764	**7.48%** — More income continues to be generated by the IRA 590™ for life.
Total Income Received:	$147,961	$191,932	**29.72%** — More income received since income began.
Death Benefit:	$234,886	$250,000	**6.43%** — More to heirs, because the IRA 590™ is never drawn down by distributions.
Tax paid by heirs:	$91,139		**$91,139** — More to heirs on the IRA 590™. The IRA 590™ passes to heirs completely tax free.
Net Death Benefit:	$143,748	$250,000	**73.92%** — More since the IRA 590™ passes completely tax free to heirs.
Total Benefits:	$291,709	$441,932	**51.50%** — More at life expectancy. In fact, the longer you live, the more valuable it becomes.

Net to Heirs: Even More if Inheritance Taxes Apply

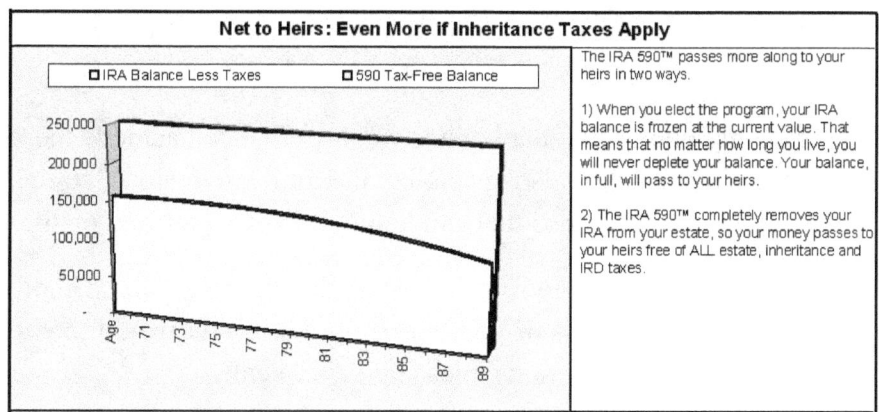

☐ IRA Balance Less Taxes   ☐ 590 Tax-Free Balance

The IRA 590™ passes more along to your heirs in two ways.

1) When you elect the program, your IRA balance is frozen at the current value. That means that no matter how long you live, you will never deplete your balance. Your balance, in full, will pass to your heirs.

2) The IRA 590™ completely removes your IRA from your estate, so your money passes to your heirs free of ALL estate, inheritance and IRD taxes.

IPA™ is a trademark of Consolpro™. The plan is only available through Consolpro™ and its agents. Any numbers used in this calculator and illustrations within this book are deemed accurate but are for illustration purposes only.

inheritance or federal estate taxes. However under the IPA™, that money passes free of all taxes. So the IPA™ is immediately worth almost 60% more.

At life expectancy—age 82—RMDs have risen to $13,736. Since age 70, the IPA™ has provided about $44,000 more in income. But because the IPA™ is an Income4Life principal preservation strategy, the death benefit is still $250,000, where the IRA has been depleted to $234,866. In addition, the IPA™ passes to heirs completely tax-free, instead of the $91,139 in IRD taxes paid on the traditional IRA. Therefore, the $250,000 is worth $135,000 more in the IPA™ than the traditional IRA in only 12 years, GUARANTEED, without increasing risk at all.

Once again, it's not what you make but what you keep that matters. And it's not magic; it's simply managing risk, fees and taxes that makes the difference.

Like any pension plan, the IPA™ can be configured many ways. It can include a long term care benefit, health insurance, life insurance...any benefit you want. And the best part about it is that if you do it right, it never costs a dime. How? By utilizing the dollars you would have paid to Uncle Sam in taxes to fund the plan!

This is only one of the many plans we have that can achieve these or similar results. We also specialize in Roth conversions, stretch IRAs and other strategies that can help with your qualified plans.

However, we could never know what direction to take without doing a careful analysis of your situation. So, if you would like to explore any of these options, please give us a call.

Receive lifetime income without giving up control of your money

This is something that only insurance companies can provide, and makes planning for retirement extraordinarily easy compared to a traditional money manager.

Long life vs. Good life

When you plan for income from your savings, you have to plan for one (or two) individuals. You don't know how long you will live, but you have to *plan for a long life,* and try to balance that against taking the maximum amount of income so you can *have a good life*!

But the two are always in conflict. Long life says you spend less. Good life says you spend more and run the risk of running out of money. So typically your advisor will tell you to take no more than 4% of your investments every year. That means if you have accumulated $1 million, you get income of $40,000 per year. And you thought you were going to be rich!

The insurance company doesn't have to do this. It knows exactly how long you will live, so it can give you the exactly correct amount of money to live the best and longest life possible. Know-So Money!

Well, it doesn't really know how long *you* will live, but it isn't dealing with just you. It is dealing with tens, maybe hundreds of thousands of individuals with needs very similar to yours. So it can calculate with scientific certainty how many people will live to what ages. And since you are in that pool with an annuity, you get to take advantage of it.

In the past you had to annuitize, or *give up your pool of money* to take advantage of this. Now, for your parents, that wasn't such a big deal. They were used to thinking of the "defined benefits": the income stream. You, however, have been taught to look at the "defined contribution": the pot of money you have invested. When you come at it from that perspective, it's much less attractive to annuitize, *even though that's the best way to maximize income.*

So once again, the industry responded with brand new strategies just for you. They came up with something called the income rider. The income rider allows you to take advantage of the insurance company's ability to provide you income based on the "law of large numbers" without giving up control of your money.

Imagine your money is divided into two pools. One pool is your "walk away balance." This is driven by the indexing we discussed earlier in this book. When the market goes up, so does your balance. When the market goes down, you are locked in, never to lose a dime. After the surrender period, you can walk away with this balance, less any withdrawals.

Now, the other pool is comprised of a source of money for lifetime income. And it grows not just based on the indexing, but also by a fixed guaranteed. That guarantee is usually in the 7-8% range, so it is guaranteed to double every 10 years. So, if you started 20 years ago with $100,000, today you would have a minimum of $400,000 *for income*, guaranteed.

Now, the insurance company uses that number to calculate your income payout. If you started at age 50, and are now age 70, your payout factor would be 5.5% (remember, your traditional planner can only give you 4%, and that isn't guaranteed). So under our scenario you get $22,000 in income guaranteed for the rest of your life, no matter how long you live and no matter what the market does, all based on an initial investment of $100,000! This is financial magic, and it's only available from annuities.

Now, assume you only collect that $22,000 for a few years, and then you die, or better yet, just change your mind. In the old model, when you had to annuitize, your money would have been gone, and your money would have died with you.

Not anymore. Under this model, we go back to that other pool of money, that "walk away balance." That has been continuing to accumulate the entire time you have been taking withdrawals. So, you just deduct the total amount of the withdrawals from your walk away balance, and you get to...you got it...walk away with the balance!

Okay, one more thing before we move on. What if the "walk away balance" out performs the guaranteed rate of 7%-8% on the income account. Do you get to take advantage of that?

You bet. The income account can be more, but never less than the walk away balance. So, if you have remarkable years like we have over the past several years and the annuity performs very well on the index side, you take advantage of that. Every year the balance is reviewed. If the income account is less than the walk away, it gets adjusted upwards to the walk away balance, and then starts accumulating at 7%-8% all over again. Here is how this would all look on a chart:

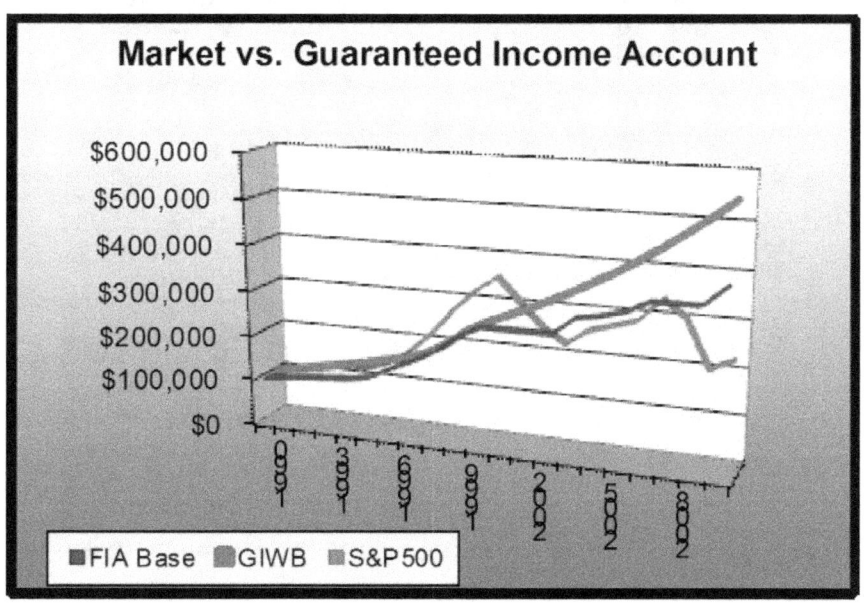

Pay less than 2% in taxes on your investment income. Here's how.

Illustration assumes client requires $12,000 per year of Tax-advantaged income from $200,000 non-qualified funds.

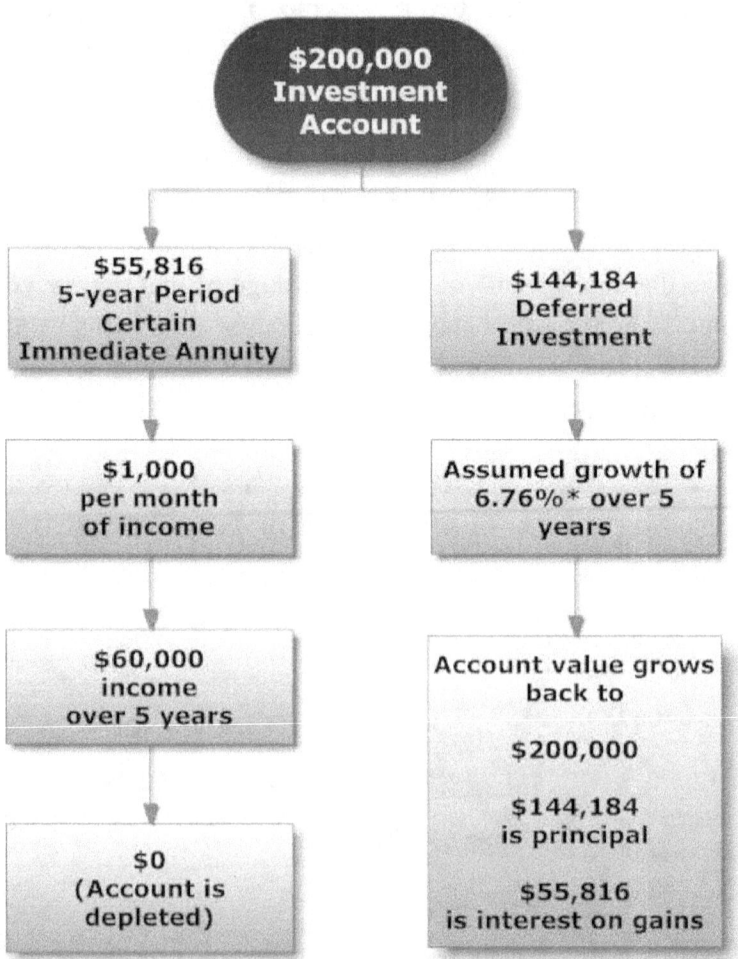

Here's a case where a traditional immediate annuity makes all kinds of sense. By taking a chunk of your investment money and annuitizing it over a five year period, you not only maximize income, you eliminate volatility in your income stream and dramatically reduce taxes.

Annuity payouts have something called an exclusion ratio that dramatically reduces the amount of taxes paid: in this case only about 5%-6%.

That means that during the time you are taking income from this plan, you are not only paying much lower taxes on your investment income, but your other taxes could be minimized as well. You might even find that taxes on Social Security income could be eliminated altogether, and your tax bracket much lower.

But that's not the only benefit. It also provides an income stream over the next five years that is not subject to the whims of the market. If there is a down period like we have had over the past few years, your income remains steady and intact. Plus, since your investment dollars are in longer-term strategies (five years or more) you have a longer period of time to recover from down times before you have to take your money out for income.

This is much better than having to sell off shares when the market is down just so you can live. That can cripple your entire retirement plan for the rest of your life, because once shares are gone, they're gone; unavailable to appreciate when the market recovers.

Or, if you are like most of our clients, perhaps the longer-term money is in a Fixed Index Annuity where there is no downside and no risk of loss! And, because you don't need it for a long period of time (five to ten years depending on how the plan is crafted), surrender periods and surrender charges are taken completely out of the picture.

This is one of our very favorite strategies, and is one of the most popular among our clients. It provides lower taxes, more dependable income and safety; three things today's retirees really value.

Eliminate probate Fees and State Inheritance taxes

Many people believe that if you have a will then you will avoid probate. This is the exact opposite of the truth; probate is, in fact, the execution of the will. The will instructs the court how it should distribute the "probative property." Probative property is defined as that property which is not under joint ownership, or that which is not contractually promised.

Since life insurance and annuities have a designated beneficiary, they are "contractually promised" upon the death of the owner. That means that they pass directly to the beneficiary, outside of probate. This is a very good thing, but it's very important to get the beneficiary designations right when executing these contracts.

It's crucial to understand that beneficiary designations ALWAYS win over other documentation, such as wills and trust documents. Therefore if you have an old insurance policy that designates an ex-spouse, or a former business partner, or whomever as the beneficiary, that's who it will go to *regardless of what your will says.*

We have found this to be a problem more than once. In fact we know of one case where a man forgot to take his ex-spouse off his retirement plan at work, and when he died his wife of nearly 20 years got not one dime of the retirement they had worked so hard to accumulate during their marriage. It all went...not to his ex-spouse, as she predeceased him, but to her children who he never even knew. And the court upheld the decision, ruling that the beneficiary was king.

So, if you haven't done it already, perhaps now would be a great time to have your beneficiary designations reviewed. This is a service we offer at no charge. Give us a call, and we will schedule a time to go over them for you.

10 Most Common Objections

1. "I don't want to tie up my money."

We get it. Where is the most liquid place you can think of to put your money? Money market accounts? Checking? Savings? Your mattress? Why don't you put of all your money in these locations? <u>Because you need a return that will grow your money and fight inflation. You may also need an income that these low or no -yield accounts can't give.</u>

"By the way, where is your money now?" I often ask. If your answer is "in the market," then you're violating your own liquidity principle. Bear with me. I realize you can sell anytime you want...

But if you needed your money any time between 2008 and 2009, how much could you have gotten? 50%? 60%? Less? On $100,000 let's say he sent you $50,000 (which is all that was left due to market volatility). You called him up to tell him you received the $50,000 and ask how long it will be before you get the other $50,000. He informed you that if you want the second $50,000 you had to return the first $50,000 and then wait an unspecified time... and <u>maybe</u> you will get it back. In other words, you may have little or no liquidity. That's Hope-So Money.

With an FIA the worst your liquidity could be damaged would be to return all but about 10%-12% (<u>again – worst case – usually much lower</u>) due to surrender charges. However, you have the opportunity to take 10% annually with no penalty, adding up to withdrawing your entire original premium in 10 years (or a little longer, depending on your return, and whether the 10% is calculated on the original premium every year or the new account value). Do you have a plan in place to spend your entire principal in ten years?

So, with a fixed annuity you know up front what the worst case scenario will be. And because you know the facts without a doubt, you can do actual planning. Know-So Money!

2. "I don't get all the upside – caps and participation rates are limiting."

It's true that you don't get all the upside with an FIA. However, it is not a disadvantage to get some of the up and none of the down compared to what most people get. Actually, with your diversified portfolio, not only are you not getting all the up, but you are participating in all of the down. Personally, I would rather get some of the up and none of the down than to get some of the up and all of the down. (Some of my clients got over 10% in the last couple of years—with no risk. How did you do?)

3. "I don't like surrender charges."

Surrender charges are voluntary and self-imposed if more than a 10% penalty-free withdrawal is made in a given year. Let's say you had a charge as high as 12% (worst case) for an amount taken above the 10% penalty-free withdrawal. Let's use the example of a $20,000 withdrawal from a $100,000 account. The first $10,000 is penalty free. The second 10,000 withdrawal would incur a 12% charge ($1,200). $1,200 is 1.2% of your $100,000 account. Let's also assume that you made 8% on your account's growth in the same year. Effectively, what you have done is to withdraw 20% of the account and reduced your 8% interest to 6.8% as a result of the fee. I tell people in the rare cases when they need more than 10% to go ahead and take it. It's not the end of the world.

I understand printed surrender charges, which are disclosed before you buy an annuity, seem scary. "What if I need my money and I have to pay a fee to get it?" is likely what you are thinking. But…have you ever signed a prospectus that basically said you can lose your shirt, but because there is not a printed schedule of the market's volatility charges and because you think everybody else is doing it, it must be okay?

I have had people come into my office and show me statements with as much as 50% losses; but because it was not in print in the form of a penalty schedule before they bought, they bought anyway. I have never seen a fixed annuity with a 50% surrender charge. Surrender charges are completely within your control and don't come into play unless you make that choice. Further, the market's volatility "charges" happen to you involuntarily. One more thing…there is such a thing as a Fixed Indexed Annuity that delivers 100% liquidity of the initial premium any time you want it, with no surrender charges!

4. "My broker doesn't like fixed annuities."

No kidding. Approximately $20 billion a year is flowing out of brokerage accounts into index annuities. Not only doesn't your broker like them, the whole investment community doesn't like them.

It shouldn't surprise you that your broker or anyone else doesn't like anything he views as having the possibility of taking your accounts away from him or her. It's like ripping the braces off his kid's teeth (or that's the way he/she may see it!) I have not met many brokers who don't sell FIAs who actually understand them themselves, much less have the ability to be able to fairly and accurately explain them to their clients. In any event, who are you trying to please? Yourself or your broker?

5. "My broker told me your commissions are too high."

This one is truly amusing. I don't mind telling you that my commission for the longest term and highest paying contract I have averages about .6% (point six percent) per year in compensation. More often than not, the broker who is telling you not to buy because of high commissions is in all likelihood being paid as much as 1.5%-2% per year, or two to three times what I get paid *plus two to three times that in hidden fees!**

Further, all these fees are deducted from your funds. That means whether you make money or lose money, YOU will pay the fees! So, if you have $100,000 in the market you paid around $30,000-$40,000 in fees over the past 10 years!

With a Fixed Index Annuity, the commission is paid directly by the insurance company. **Not a penny comes out of your funds as long as you abide by the terms of the contract**, unless you elect additional benefits available for a fully disclosed charge. 100% of your money is working and growing for you. The only time you would ever be charged is if you take your money out early, in which case the insurance company asks that you help cover the charges caused by the early withdrawal (surrender charges).

6. "The index calculations don't include dividends."

It's true. Again, you won't get all the up. However, can you give me an example of something that includes or pays dividends that has no risk to your principal or previously earned gains? It's not a perfect world, and I admit I'm not offering perfection; but I remind you again that you already own an imperfect investment… and one where you could lose your shirt (not possible with an FIA!).

*Source: Pryor, Anna; *The Hidden Costs of Mutual Funds*; The Wall Street Journal Online, March 1, 2010

7. "My broker says annuities aren't appropriate for qualified funds such as IRAs and 401(k)s."

Remember that when anyone in the financial field—except a safe-money planner—refers to annuities they are almost always referring to variable annuities. And I would agree completely that variable annuities aren't appropriate for qualified funds...on any other funds for that matter. But not so with fixed and fixed index annuities!

It's true that from a tax standpoint it's a wash; but what about safety, liquidity, and guaranteed income? All of these should be considered as well. When looking at the complete picture most people agree that it makes sense to have some money in an FIA. This product is not likely to duplicate any other investment you have. We are all taught to diversify, and an FIA is a great way to do it. Think about safely linking to the horsepower of 500 stocks represented in the S&P 500 as compared to owning a couple of stocks directly. This is much greater diversification.

8. "Can I trust an insurance company with my money?"

I find it interesting that people trust insurance companies with insuring their homes, cars, health <u>and life</u>, but not their nest eggs and future income (and then they don't think twice about putting nearly all of their savings at risk where they not only know they could lose it, but most often have lost it in the past) If we can feel okay about trusting them (insurance companies) with all that we do, then shouldn't we be okay with having them insure our nest eggs and income? Reread the section on the Legal Reserve System, and you will see why these contracts are so safe.

9. "I don't believe there is enough horsepower in an FIA, and I can make more in mutual funds."

We already know that the best way to grow money is to never have to make up for a loss, even for one year. Adding interest every year that has been generated from stock market indices, or a bond index or the fixed account <u>to the highest amount you have ever had,</u> minus your voluntary withdrawals will compete very favorably over time with a volatile market that <u>continuously takes back previously-earned gains</u>.

Some people call the first ten years of this century the "Lost Decade" because many put up the capital, took the risk and had nothing to show for it. Not annuity owners! If you had been in an FIA for the same period of time, the story would have been much different and vastly better. In fact, we had some clients that doubled, or even tripled their money over that 10 year period. Did you?

Think of the market as a powerful jet plane flying at 500 mph into a 600 mph head-wind. Yes it's powerful, but how far are you really going to go? Now, think of the annuity as a 300 mph nonstop bullet train with no head wind to fight. Which is going to get you there faster?

10. "The fees are too high."

That's true, if we are discussing variable annuities, which most brokers deal in. However, with *fixed annuities* there are no fees unless an extra benefit is added on. The insurance company earns a spread between the gross of the bond portfolio's yield, which they manage, and the net is credited to your account. This spread is similar to how banks make money and typically ranges around 2% annually. From this spread the insurance company pays the agent, covers the insurance company's expenses and returns a profit to its shareholders.

The difference is that a spread is not taken from your existing account balance. So in a year where the annuity credits zero growth due to a flat or declining market, the FIA owner gets a true zero - not zero minus 2-4 ½% in management fees, which is what happens on brokerage accounts and variable annuities (or even a loss minus 2-4 ½% !), adding insult to injury!

In Summary

I know there are many unanswered questions that you probably still have. This book was not intended to answer them all. That's why we are here. Is an annuity the answer for you? I have no idea. But you probably don't either, and unless you have at least considered it as a possibility, how could you possibly know? Rather than just take these very powerful, safe, and dependable sources of Know-So Money and guaranteed income off the table because your broker or barber doesn't like them, why not take a look? After all, how can you know what you should do if you don't know what you can do?

And Finally...

Like what you read in this booklet? Get much more from my book, **"Safe Harbors That Can Reduce Taxes, Remove Risk, and Protect Your Retirement."**

You can get this online through Amazon.com.

Or we are happy to provide you with a complimentary copy. Just call us at 603-881-8811 or log into our website at www.FreeMoneyGuys.com and request your copy today!

Thanks!

So, in Mr. Spock's immortal words, "May you live long and prosper!"

About Stephen Kelley

Stephen J. Kelley, CSA®, is a Registered Investment Advisor, a respected financial and business consultant and founder of Safety First Financial Planners. For a quarter century he has helped individuals and organizations raise money, manage their finances and achieve best business and financial practices. A Certified Senior Advisor®, Steve has for the past 10 years specialized in working with seniors and boomers who are either in or preparing for retirement, through his own financial planning practice and through financial planning workshops that he teaches at colleges throughout New England.

Steve is the author of the book, "Safe Harbors That Can Reduce Taxes, Remove Risk and Protect Your Retirement," available on Amazon.com. A former journalist, his work has been published in numerous books, newspapers and magazines. Along with his partner Mark Perkins, Steve can be heard several times a week on the regionally syndicated "Free Money Radio Hour." In addition he writes a column, "Main Street Money," for his hometown newspaper, the Nashua Telegraph and the Lowell Sun.

Steve often says that his proudest achievement is that not one of his Safe Money clients has ever lost a dime due to market volatility or risk. He has built his practice on the premise, "The most important thing you can do for a retiree is to keep their money safe. Everything else is secondary."

Steve is the proud recipient of the **2013 and 2014 BBB Perfect Score Award** as well as the **2011 and 2012 New Hampshire Magazine 5-Star Professional Wealth Manager** award. Fewer than seven percent of wealth managers receive this award each year, based on a survey 65,000 high net worth individuals and 3,000 planning professionals in New Hampshire.

www.ingramcontent.com/pod-product-compliance
Lightning Source LLC
Chambersburg PA
CBHW070718180526
45167CB00004B/1532